wish you
ch love for
the environment
Many Blessings
Loise Ross

Tha
Mary Tyler Moore

Sacred Woods

Of The Highlands Plateau
And The Southern Appalachians

Mary Kay Moore

Focus on Preservation and Conservation

Dedicated to my Mother and all my relations, past, present and future

Edited by Lexie Ross

Library of Congress Control Number: 2002110873

ISBN: 1-881851-18-4

Mary Kay Moore, P.O. Box 1823, Highlands, NC 28741   marykaymoorem@aol.com

Printed in the United States of America on acid-free paper.

FOREWORD

In this selection of color prints, photographer Mary Kay Moore has captured the natural beauty of the Highlands Plateau in North Carolina. This region has long been acclaimed for its deep gorges, majestic rivers, spectacular waterfalls, and scenic views. Founded as a summer resort in the 1870s, the town of Highlands has always attracted an unusually wealthy and well-educated group of citizens. This small, isolated mountain village boasts the first public library in North Carolina: the still extant Hudson Library. It also offers unexpectedly rich cultural opportunities, such as a summer playhouse, an art museum and a chamber music series. Highlands also fostered the first land trust in the state and is home to one of the oldest biological field stations in North America: the 75-year-old Highlands Biological Station.

Highlands and its immediate surroundings are arguably the most biologically significant area in the entire Appalachian Mountains. Located near the crest of the Blue Ridge on a high plateau at an elevation of 4,118 feet, the town advertises itself as "the highest incorporated town east of the Rocky Mountains." It lies just west of the main drainage divide of the eastern part of the continent. Surrounding peaks on the Blue Ridge exceed 5,000 feet in elevation. The Cowee Mountains lie to the north and beyond them, the Balsams. To the northwest are the Great Smoky Mountains, with the Nantahalas to the west, across the Little Tennessee Valley. South and southeast of the Highlands Plateau is a series of river gorges, with the highest waterfalls in eastern North America. These rivers include the Cullasaja, Toxaway, Horsepasture, Thompson, Whitewater and Chattooga, which has been designated a National Wild and Scenic River and which flows through the Ellicott Rock Wilderness Area a short distance south of Highlands. Much of the land in the vicinity is part of the Nantahala National Forest. Sections of the Pisgah, Chattahoochee (Georgia), and Sumter (South Carolina) National Forests are nearby.

The Highlands area is characterized by relatively mild temperatures, with summers being especially pleasant, as daily maxima rarely exceed 80° F. Precipitation is higher than at any other site in eastern North America, averaging 80 to 100 inches annually. Under these conditions, we essentially have a "temperate rain forest." But the location of Highlands near the southern edge of the Blue Ridge affords easy access to a great variety of other plant communities over a gradient in elevation of more than 3,000 feet, extending from oak-pine and bottomland hardwood forests of the Piedmont, through the mesophytic cove forests of the Appalachian slopes, to the grass and heath balds and the spruce-fir forests on the summits of the higher peaks. The area is renowned for the diversity of its plant and animal life, which has been studied intensively by researchers at the Highlands Biological Station for more than 75 years.

It is these unique features of the Highlands Plateau that Mary Kay has captured in her photographs: hugh, ancient trees shaped over the centuries by wind and sun; landscapes worn by water (but never by glaciation) over the millenia; and the incredibly diverse plants, animals, and fungi. These photographs celebrate a superlative natural area -- the highest, wettest, most diverse forests in eastern North America. They are also an invitation to others who, like Mary Kay, are naturalists and preservationists at heart to visit this incredible natural region and revel in its beauty. "Take only photographs; leave only footprints."

Robert Wyatt, Executive Director
Highlands Biological Station
Highlands, NC

INTRODUCTION

The summer of 1992 was my first introduction to the Highlands Plateau. I was immediately captivated by the incredible beauty of the high vistas of Whiteside Mountain and the myriad rushing waterfalls, rivers, and streams which seemed to be calling my name. I felt that I had been here before and that the wilderness had opened its arms to me and held me in its scared bosom.

I was born and raised in Kentucky in a small college town where everyone knew one another. We lived on a hundred acre farm with large fields to plant and harvest. Our home was nestled between two lush tree-filled hills, one of which was three feet short of being called a mountain. My brother and I often threatened to add the three feet of dirt and rock ourselves to make it qualify. Every Saturday, we would climb that hill and dream together about traveling to far off lands and living in the mountains. When my family left the Kentucky mountains in 1966, I was determined to find the place of my imagination. Upon arriving at the Highlands Plateau, I realized I had far exceeded by dreams.

Being a descendent of naturalist and visionary John Muir, I was inspired to live in the rugged beauty of the high Sierra and Yosemite National Park. When I returned and discovered the Southern Appalachains, I didn't understand why this precious Rain Forest in the Highlands Plateau has not been set aside for a national park.

While roaming and photographing these blessed mountains, I have had many mystical experiences. Many healings have occurred that have helped me understand even more deeply the very urgent need to protect and conserve our remaining green spaces. Our rapidly dwindling trees are the lungs of the planet. They bring the rain. In mindlessly cutting them for our homes and commerce, we have created the drought and fires we are currently suffering. It is our obligation to preserve the quality of air and life for future generations and to conserve the natural spaces for the spiritual healing and soothing renewal they provide we humans and all living things.

Jon Kabet Zinn said it best...*"Mountains are sacred places. People have always sought spiritual guidance and renewal in and among them. Rising above all else on our planet, they beckon and overwhelm with their sheer presence. Mountains are the places of visions, where one can touch the panoramic scale of the natural world and its intersection with life's fragile, but tenacious rootings."*

With the publishing of this book, my goal is to awaken and encourage others to view the earth our Mother, as a sacred place in which we have been given this responsibility of stewardship...to realize that it is now imperative that we preserve and nourish the two dwindling rain forests that are left in America.

Mary Kay Moore

"Oh, these vast, calm
measureless mountainous days
which open a thousand windows
to show us God."

John Muir

WHITESIDE MOUNTAIN, Highlands, NC

Scared Nature

Whose soul is not touched by the magic prelude of the morning mist, by the other worldly dimensions of a majestic mountain view adorned by God's golden lilac dawns and sundowns?

Whose heart does not leap with glee at the whispering motor of a hummingbird's wings, or purr at the ecstatic beauty of the myriad flowers?

And, whose spirit does not still in a wooded cavern or a mirrored mountain lake, or a stream glistening in the summer sun?

Who of us are not awed by autumn's lavish harvest of colors or a winter's blanket of new morning snow?

We are all a part of this divine earthly membrane. We are all touched with wonder at this our mutual existence.

But, do not forget that this delicate paradise is a gift. Let our gratitude be shown by our caring.

Lexie Ross

CULLASAJA RIVER, *Highlands/Franklin, NC*

HAY SCENTED FERN, Cashiers, NC

4

FALL FOLIAGE, *Highlands, NC*

"Knowing that Nature never did betray
the heart that loved her.
Come forth into the light of things,
let Nature be your teacher."

Henry Wadsworth

MOUNTAIN LAUREL, *Satulah Mountain, Highlands, NC*

"A voice of greeting from the wind was sent.

The mists enfolded me with soft white arms;

The birds did sing to lap me in content.

The rivers wave their charms --

And every little daisy in the grass

Did look up in my face and smile

to see me pass!"

Richard Henry Stoddard

SATULAH TRAIL, Satulah Mountain, Highlands, NC

SATULAH SUMMIT, Highlands, NC

10

DANCING LAUREL, Satulah Mountain, Highlands, NC

Love the planet into peace.
Smile into the eyes of your unknown brother
And tuck a piece of his heart into yours.

Embrace the planet with your love,
Cherish the wisdom of the trees.
And know that the beauty of the flowers will never
be excelled.

Pray for the healing of the earth.
Strive toward the cleansing of the water and the
sweetening of the air.
Allow the children to be spared by your caring.

Swallow the pearl of immortality.
Unlike the mystical dragon
Allow not the glitter of your existence,
to dim the radiance of your spirit.
Show your father the questing of your soul.

Lexie Ross

HORSE COVE, Highlands, NC

LAKE SEQUOYAH, Highlands, NC

14

CULLASAJA FALLS, Franklin, NC

"Another glorious day in which one seems to be dissolved and absorbed and sent pulsing onward we know not where. Life seems neither long nor short, and we take no more heed to save time or make haste than do the trees and stars. This is true freedom, a good practical sort of immortality ..."

John Muir

UPPER WARDEN'S FALLS, *Pantertown, Cashiers, NC*

BRIDAL VEIL FALLS, Highlands, NC

SLIPPERY ROCK FALLS, *Cashiers, NC*

"We still think in terms of conquest. We still haven't become mature enough to think of ourselves as only a tiny part of a vast and incredible universe. Man's attitude toward nature is today critically important simply because we have now acquired a fateful power to alter and destroy nature.

Rachel Carson

SEQUOYAH FALLS, Highlands, NC

LAKE GLENVILLE, NC

22

SOUTH TRAIL TO SUNSET ROCK, Highlands, NC

KELSEY TRAIL, Highlands, NC

24

CHATTOOGA FALLS, Cashiers, NC

"These beautiful days must enrich all my life. They do not exist as mere pictures ..., but they saturate themselves into every part of the body and live always.

John Muir

SILVER RUN FALLS, Cashiers, NC

"Our ideals, laws and customs should be based
on the proposition that each generation becomes
the custodian rather than the absolute
owner of our resources and each generation
has the obligation to pass this inheritance
on to the future"

Charles Lindberg

UPPER CHATTOOGA FALLS, *Cashiers, NC*

SUNSET ROCK , Highlands, NC

30

BAMBOO FOREST, *Chattooga River, NC*

NORTHERN RED OAK, *The Mountain, Scaly, NC*

32

LAKE GLENVILLE, NC

TURTLEBACK FALLS, Horsepasture River, Toxaway, NC

34

DRY FALLS, Cullassaja River, Highlands, NC

TRILLIUM, *Whiteside Mountain, Cashiers, NC*

36

WHITEWATER FALLS, NC

The world turns softly
Not to spill its lakes and rivers,
The water is held in its arms,
And the sky is held in the water.
What is water, that pours
silver,
And can hold the sky?

Hilda Conkling

RAINBOW FALLS, Toxaway, NC

SATULAH SUMMIT, Highlands, NC

FLOMS BARN, Glenville, NC

FLOMS BARN, *Glennville, NC*

42

WHITESIDE MOUNTAIN, Highlands, NC

WHITESIDE MOUNTAIN, Cashiers, NC

FLY FISHERMAN, *Chattooga River, NC*

WHITESIDE MOUNTAIN, Highlands, NC (Courtesy of Martha McMillan}

46

MULTI-STEMMED HICKORY TREE, *Kelsey Trail,*
Highlands, NC

Blue Ridge Spring

Enchanting spring! God calls all of,
his blooming angels to decorate life's
new beginnings. My heart is elated
with the celebration of love and color.

Even the birds in their morning
spring symphonies announce
the golden pink dawns.

I am filled with gratitude
and peace.

Lexie Ross

RHODODENDRON, *Highlands, NC*

LITTLE CANADA, NC

50

"The whole territory on the top of the mountain shall be most holy."
Ezekial 43:12

STAINED GLASS
Church of the Incarnation,
Highlands, NC

ACKNOWLEDGEMENTS

Many thanks to those who have helped and encouraged me along the way: Dotson Adams, Dixie Barton, Moyna Monroe, Martha McMillan, Jane Clair, Hunter Coleman, Rufus and Marion Broadaway, Mary Thompson, Grigsby Arnette, Ran Ransdel, Dr. Robert Wyatt, Ann Baird, Mary Adair Leslie, Mark Brennen, Jenny Crager, Karen Early, Rita Bradt, Irene and Frankie Hicks, Gene and Billy Lytle, Billy, Garnetta and Scot Fouch, Roberta Early, Patty Brown, Dr Randy Wells, Bob and Carol Messer, Hazel Fugate, Jack and Becky, Sally, Sandy and Joe Carter, Jack and Lois Holly, Dr. Stephan and "Gigi" Graham Tchividjian and family, Steve and Anna Brown, Dr. John Toms, Ken Wackes, Guy Metzger, the Ellis', Early's, Ginny Harris, Dick Strain, the Moore's, Carters, Whites, V. Jane Windsor, Mary Ann Marshall, Dr. Catherine J. Foote, Sherry and Bob Yates, Nina and Trish Summers, Roger Carter and especially to my nieces and nephews Jonathan, Summer, Michelle, Kristopher, Thomas, Dawson, Kristen, Lacy, Melissa, Darrel and Kim Ann.

Special thanks to Ronnie, Robbie, Mike and my faithful companion, Max.

I am indebted to Lexie Ross for her editing expertise.

In memory of Ray Moore, my father, and nephew Quintin Ray Moore who left too soon. Also, Ouida Messer, Lyda Carter and Betty Wallin.

My thanks to you who love nature, *WE CAN MAKE A DIFFERENCE!*

Mary Kay Moore